PERFECT PIGS

❧ An Introduction to Manners ❧

Marc Brown and Stephen Krensky

Joy Street Books

Little, Brown and Company
Boston   Toronto   London

For the sow sisters
Colleen and Kim

HC: 10 9 8 7 6 5

PB: 10 9 8 7 6

Library of Congress Cataloging in Publication Data

Brown, Marc Tolon.
  Perfect pigs.

  Summary: A simple introduction to good manners to use with family, friends, at school, during meals, with pets, on the phone, during games, at parties, and in public places.
  1. Etiquette for children and youth. [1. Etiquette]
I. Krensky, Stephen. II. Title.
BJ1857.C5B67 1983   395'.122   83-746
ISBN 0-316-11079-5
ISBN 0-316-11080-9 (pbk.)

JOY STREET BOOKS
ARE PUBLISHED BY
LITTLE, BROWN AND COMPANY (INC.)

AHS

*Published simultaneously in Canada
by Little, Brown & Company (Canada) Limited*

PRINTED IN THE UNITED STATES OF AMERICA

Contents

At All Times

Say "Please" when you ask for something . . .

and "Thank you" when you get it.

Think about and respect the feelings of everyone.

Clean up after yourself.

Take care of the property of others, as well as your own.

Remember that you can't always get your own way.

5

Around the House

Wipe your feet before coming inside.

6

Knock on the door before entering a room.

Play quietly if someone is sleeping.

NEATNESS AND CONSIDERATION ARE MY TRADEMARKS.

7

With Your Family

Ask to borrow things,
and return them when you're done.

Let others know you care about them.

Use words to solve arguments
instead of fighting.

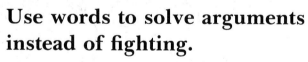

Help out with chores.

On the Telephone

When making a call, give your name, then ask for the person you wish to speak to.

When answering a call . . .

Don't call friends too early in the morning . . .
or too late at night.

When someone can't come to the phone . . .

11

During Meals

Wash your hands before eating.

Ask politely for food that you can't reach.

When you sit down, put your napkin on your lap.
Use it to wipe your hands and mouth.

Cut your food into bite-size pieces.

Don't play with your food.

Don't talk with your mouth full.

ENOUGH TALK. WHEN DO WE EAT?

13

Use the right utensil or dish.

14